SandCastle 2

The Senses

Sense of Sight

Carey Molter

ABDO
Publishing Company

Published by SandCastle™, an imprint of ABDO Publishing Company, 4940 Viking Drive, Edina, Minnesota 55435.

Printed in the United States.

Photo credits: Comstock, Corbis Images, Image 100, PhotoDisc

Library of Congress Cataloging-in-Publication Data

Molter, Carey, 1973-
Sense of sight / Carey Molter.
p. cm. -- (The senses)
Includes index.
ISBN 1-57765-626-1
1. Vision--Juvenile literature. [1. Vision. 2. Senses and sensation.] I. Title.

QP475.7 .M64 2001
612.8'4--dc21

2001022903

The SandCastle concept, content, and reading method have been reviewed and approved by a national advisory board including literacy specialists, librarians, elementary school teachers, early childhood education professionals, and parents.

Let Us Know

After reading the book, SandCastle would like you to tell us your stories about reading. What is your favorite page? Was there something hard that you needed help with? Share the ups and downs of learning to read. We want to hear from you! To get posted on the Abdo Publishing Company Web site, send us email at:

sandcastle@abdopub.com

About SandCastle™

Nonfiction books for the beginning reader

- Basic concepts of phonics are incorporated with integrated language methods of reading instruction. Most words are short, and phrases, letter sounds, and word sounds are repeated.
- Readability is determined by the number of words in each sentence, the number of characters in each word, and word lists based on curriculum frameworks.
- Full-color photography reinforces word meanings and concepts.
- "Words I Can Read" list at the end of each book teaches basic elements of grammar, helps the reader recognize the words in the text, and builds vocabulary.
- Reading levels are indicated by the number of flags on the castle.

Look for more SandCastle books in these three reading levels:

Level 1
(one flag)

Grades Pre-K to K
5 or fewer words per page

Level 2
(two flags)

Grades K to 1
5 to 10 words per page

Level 3
(three flags)

Grades 1 to 2
10 to 15 words per page

Our senses tell us what is going on around us.

Sight is one of our five senses.

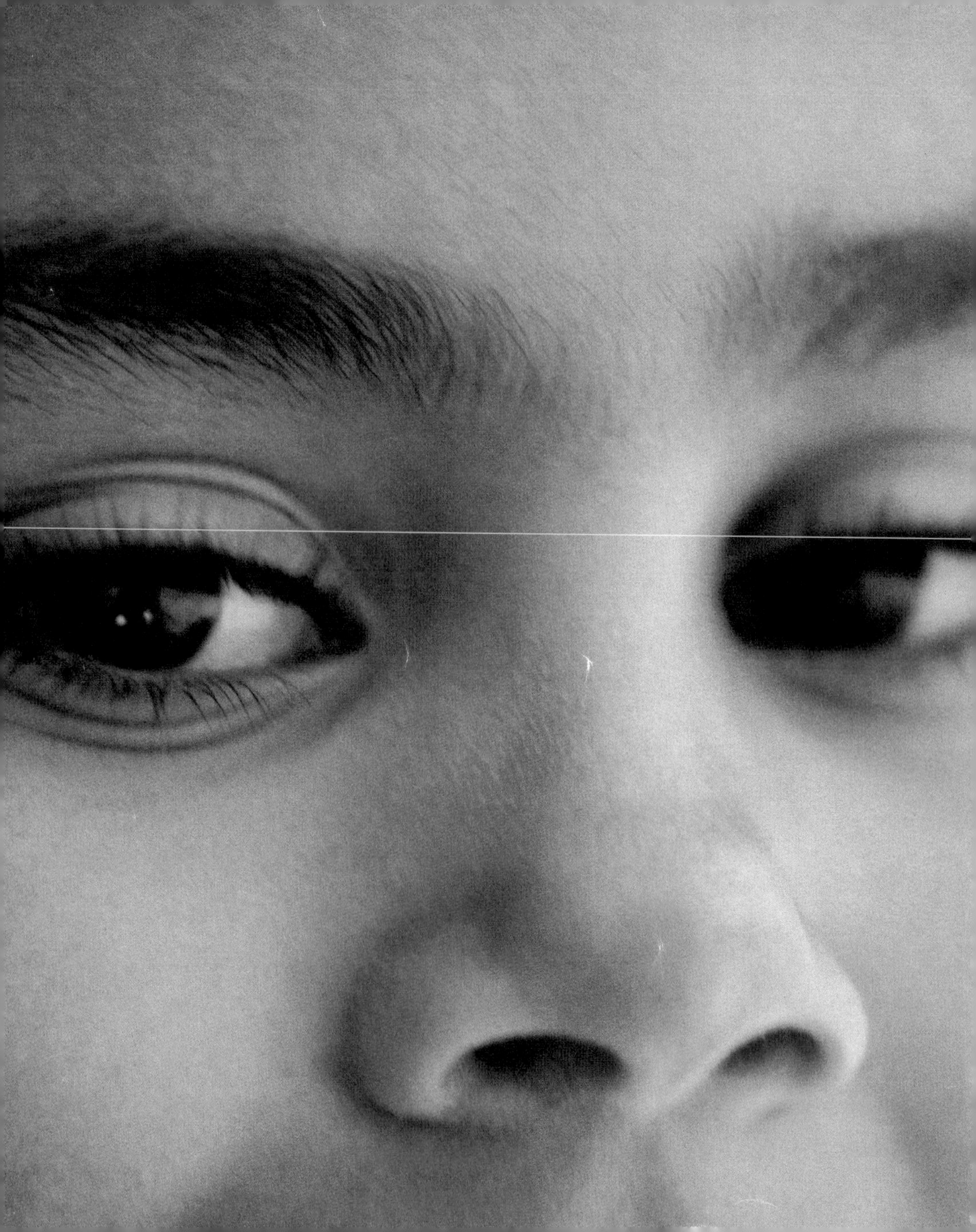

Sight is how we know what something looks like.

Carla uses her sight to see how Victor is feeling.

Sight shows Jared and his friends where they are going.

STOP

Sight helps Ann keep others safe.

Her sense of sight shows Meg where the ball is.

BIRTHDAY

We see lots of shapes and colors with our eyes.

What different shapes and colors do you see here?

Words I Can Read

Nouns

A noun is a person, place, or thing

ball (BAWL) p. 17
sense (SENSS) p. 17
sight (SITE) pp. 7, 9, 11, 13, 15, 17

Plural Nouns

A plural noun is more than one person, place, or thing

colors (KUHL-urz) pp. 19, 21
eyes (EYEZ) p. 19
senses (SENSS-ez) pp. 5, 7
friends (FRENDZ) p. 13
shapes (SHAYPSS) pp. 19, 21

Proper Nouns

A proper noun is the name of a person, place, or thing

Ann (AN) p. 15
Carla (KAR-luh) p. 11
Jared (JAIR-ed) p. 13
Meg (MEG) p. 17
Victor (VIK-tor) p. 11

Verbs

A verb is an action or being word

are (AR) p. 13
do (DOO) p. 21
is (IZ) pp. 5, 7, 9, 11, 17
feeling(FEEL-ing) p. 11
going (GOH-ing) pp. 5, 13
helps (HELPSS) p. 15
keep (KEEP) p. 15
know (NOH) p. 9
looks (LUKSS) p. 9
see (SEE) pp. 11, 19, 21
shows (SHOHZ) pp. 13, 17
tell (TEL) p. 5
uses (YOOZ-ez) p. 11

Adjectives

An adjective describes something

different (DIF-uhr-uhnt) p. 21
five (FIVE) p. 7
her (HUR) pp. 11, 17
his (HIZ) p. 13
lots (LOTSS) p. 19
one (WUHN) p. 7
safe (SAYF) p. 15

More About the Sense of Sight
Match the Words to their Pictures

shiny
dark
far
pupil

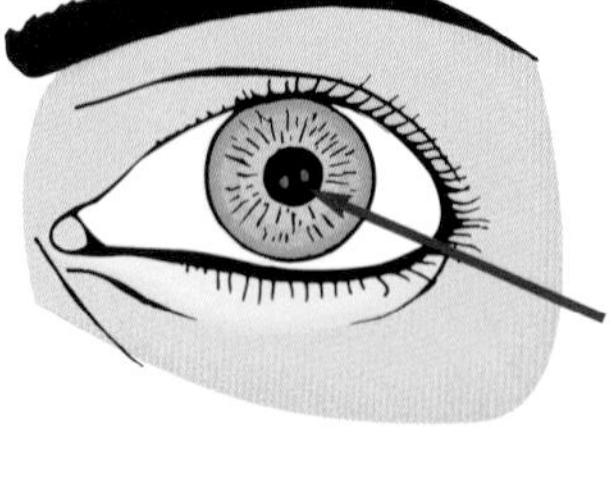